THAT'S NOT FAIR!

ELSPETH CAMPBELL MURPHY
ILLUSTRATED BY SUSAN MORRIS

Chariot Books
David C Cook Publishing Co

Chariot Books is an imprint of David C. Cook Publishing Co.
David C. Cook Publishing Co., Elgin, Illinois 60120
David C. Cook Publishing Co., Weston, Ontario

THAT'S NOT FAIR
© 1988 by Elspeth Campbell Murphy for text and GraphCom Corporation for illustrations

All rights reserved. Except for brief excerpts for review purposes, no part of this book may be reproduced or used in any form without written permission from the publisher.

Illustrated by Sue Morris; book and cover design by Marilyn Baridon

First Printing, 1988
Printed in Singapore
93 92 91 90 89 88 5 4 3 2 1

Library of Congress Cataloging-in-Publication Data
Murphy, Elspeth Campbell.
  That's not fair.
  (Proverbs to grow on)
  Summary: A child reflects on the wisdom of certain Biblical proverbs, including "Honest people will treat you fairly; the wicked only want to deceive you" and "Condemning the innocent or letting the wicked go, both are hateful to the Lord."
  1. Fairness—Juvenile literature. 2. Honesty—Juvenile literature. [1. Bible. O.T. Proverbs]
I. Morris, Susan, ill. II. Title. III. Series: Murphy, Elspeth, Campbell. Proverbs to grow on.
BJ1533.F2M87   1988   241'.699   87-35458
ISBN 1-55513-354-1

Scripture quotations on pages 15, 19, 21, 23, and 24 are from the *Good News Bible*, the Bible in Today's English Version. Copyright © American Bible Society 1966, 1971, 1976.

Scripture quotations on pages 13 and 19 are from the *Holy Bible, New International Version* copyright © 1973, 1978, 1984 International Bible Society. Used by permission of Zondervan Bible Publishers.

Why do I have all the bad luck, God? Why does everything always happen to me?

My sister gets to have her friends
over for a party.
And she gets to have a cake
with her name on it.
And she gets to open tons and tons
and *tons* of presents.
All because it's her birthday.
My birthday isn't for three whole months.
It's not fair!

My sister and her friends
went upstairs to listen to her new tapes
and hang up her new posters.
But they locked the door
and wouldn't let me in—
no matter how loud I banged.

My mother told me not to ruin
my sister's party.
I wasn't trying to ruin it, God!
I just wanted to be in it!
This was turning into the unfairest day
of my whole life.

But then things got a little better.
My mother asked my sister
if we could play with her brand-new
board game.
And my sister said yes—
even though she didn't have to.

My mother and I had to read the directions to see how to play.
People have to have directions—right, God?
Otherwise, how would we know what's fair and what's cheating?

PROVERBS 2:9

Then you will understand what is right and just and fair—every good path.

I wanted to win the game *so much*!
I thought about cheating. . . .
But—guess what, God!
I didn't!
My mom said I won fair and square.

PROVERBS 12:5

Honest people will treat you fairly; the wicked only want to deceive you.

And you know what else is fair, God?
It's fair for my sister to have a party
on her birthday.
I just said it was UNfair
because I was mad
that I have to wait so long for *my* party.

But sometimes people really *are* unfair
to other people.
And that's not following
your directions at all—is it, God?
Like just now, my friend came over to play.
And there's this big, mean kid on my street
who doesn't like my friend and me.
He said to us,
"I'm going to get you in trouble!"

PROVERBS 28:5; 19:28a

Evil men do not understand justice, but those who seek the Lord understand it fully.

There is no justice where a witness is determined to hurt someone.

Then he lied to my next-door neighbor
and told her
that my friend and I were the ones
who threw eggs at her garage.
And he lied so well my neighbor believed him!
My friend and I thought
we were going to get punished
for something we didn't even do!
Talk about unfair!

PROVERBS 17:15

Condemning the innocent or letting the wicked go—both are hateful to the Lord.

But it turned out
that the mean kid threw the eggs himself.
My sister and her friends saw him do it.
And they weren't afraid to tell
what really happened.
So I guess I don't have all the bad luck
after all, God.
My sister and her friends
stood up for my friend and me.

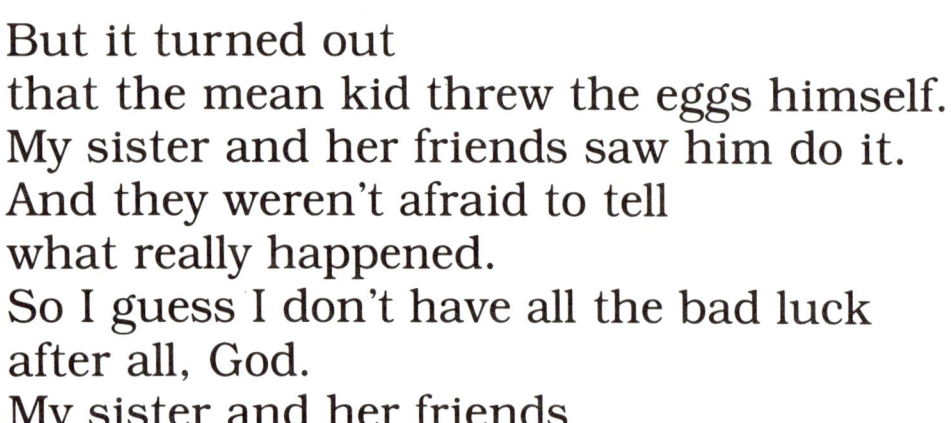

PROVERBS 31:8, 9

Speak up for people who cannot speak for themselves. Protect the rights of all who are helpless. Speak for them and be a righteous judge. Protect the rights of the poor and needy.

I *love* it when people are honest and fair.
And guess what, God!
I know you love it, too!

PROVERBS 2:7, 8

He provides help and protection for righteous, honest men. He protects those who treat others fairly, and guards those who are devoted to him.